MW01633684

CHRISTMAS
with
DICKENS

CHRISTMAS
with
DICKENS

Charles Dickens' Great-Grandsons' Gift
of A Christmas Carol Evening
Commemorating the 150th Anniversary of
A Christmas Carol

by Cedric Charles Dickens

with David and Betty Dickens

The Belvedere Press

Arlington

Originally published by Dickens Publishing, England
©1991 by Cedric Charles Dickens.

©1993 by The Belvedere Press. All rights reserved
Published by The Belvedere Press, 4908 Washington Boulevard,
Arlington, Virginia 22205

Library of Congress Cataloging-in-Publication Data
Dickens, Cedric Charles.
   Christmas with Dickens : Charles Dickens' great-grandsons' gift of
A Christmas carol evening commemorating the 150th anniversary
of A Christmas carol/ Cedric Charles Dickens with David and Betty Dickens.
      p.   cm.
   Originally published: Somerset : Dickens Pub., c 1991.
   Includes bibliographical references and index.
   ISBN 0-911057-02-1
   1. Christmas cookery. 2. Cookery, English. 3. Dickens, Charles, 1812-1870.
Christmas carol.   I. Dickens, David.   II. Dickens, Betty.   III. Dickens, Charles,
1812-1870.   Christmas carol.   1993.
   IV. Title.
   TX739.2.C45D53   1993   93-39711
   641.5'68 -- dc20   CIP

The Dickens family recipes in this book have not been tested by
The Belvedere Press.

ISBN 0-911057-02-1

Third Printing   10 9 8 7 6 5 4 3
Printed in the United States of America

To Murray Callaghan

*with thanks for that first wonderful
Christmas Carol dinner for Ed German
and his friends in the Dickens Inn,
Philadelphia — the perfect setting*

Contents

(Continued on following page)

List of Illustrations

(Continued on following page)

Preface

My very dear friends,

One hundred fifty years ago, Charles Dickens wrote *A Christmas Carol*. At the time he was only thirty-one years old. Bothered by the plight of the poor and the less fortunate, he set upon writing "a little Christmas book" in October 1843.

Feverishly he worked, often writing as he walked the streets of London until sunrise, composing as he went along the memorable characters of Scrooge, Tiny Tim, Bob Cratchit and others.

A Christmas Carol was published on December 19, 1843. Since that day, people have responded to its message: the true meaning of Christmas.

Charles Dickens was my great-grandfather. He read *A Christmas Carol* to his family, laughing and crying in all the right places. I heard my grandfather, Sir Henry Dickens, read *A Christmas Carol* to a family audience of about a hundred or so. I was so young, the only thing I remember to this day is when he got to that heart-searing part where Tiny Tim might die, tears were pouring down his cheeks, while he nearly lost his false teeth! I did hear him luckily after that.

To this day, world-wide, somebody is writing about Dickens, talking about him, making a film about him, or producing another TV program.

His *Christmas Carol* continues to give people enormous pleasure. The Ford's Theatre in Washington, D.C., the Missouri Repertory Company in Kansas City, the Guthrie in Minneapolis, and the Alliance in Atlanta present it on stage as a cherished holiday tradition.

Dickens festivals from England to Galveston, Texas and Franklin, Tennessee attract thousands of people over an entire weekend. It's magic, absolutely magic!

Philadelphia's Strawbridge and Clothier store has a lifesize *Christmas Carol* creation every year after Thanksgiving. It's fabulous! Both young and old, laugh and cry as Charles Dickens wanted them to over this wonderful story.

The more research I do into the life and times of my revered great-grandfather, the more fun I have. American friends unearth fascinating facts and send clippings to me. It seems that former First Lady Eleanor Roosevelt read aloud from the *Carol* each year after her family unwrapped Christmas presents. *The Tonight Show* host Jay Leno tries to gauge his life by his favorite line from *A Christmas Carol* —that no man could keep Christmas as well as Ebenezer Scrooge.

Deeply grateful for the world-wide affection for Charles Dickens and personally appreciative for having inherited his love of people, I wanted to create something special to thank him and people in this 150th anniversary year. My cousin, David, also a great-grandson, and his wife Betty joined with me to create *Christmas with Dickens.*

In this book, we have not attempted to emulate Charles Dickens' genius. Instead, we joyously present our book as a framework within which families, friends, church groups, and business colleagues can create their own wonderfully magical *Christmas Carol* evening.

Our book includes Dickens' letters to friends as he wrote *A Christmas Carol.* We selected line engravings from Victorian-period editions of the book. We gathered family recipes that have come to us through the years. We edited the *Carol* staves to twenty-eight minutes of reading aloud. *Christmas with Dickens'* cover design and size are inspired by the original *Christmas Carol*.

Whether your *Carol* evening is in your home dining area, a church hall, or at a full-scale banquet, we wish you a warm memorable evening. Our hope is that your *Christmas with Dickens* will become a treasured part of your holiday season.

Allow me to close with my favourite *Carol* quote: "There is nothing in the world so irresistibly contagious as laughter and good humour."

Bless you,

Cedric Charles Dickens

North Cadbury
Somerset, England

Acknowledgements

Heartfelt gratitude goes to Nancy and Sherman Poland, lovely friends in Washington, D.C., who introduced us to The Belvedere Press;

to its publisher, Caroline Jackson, whose Dickens event at Carroll Hall gave me the incredible thrill of speaking where my great-grandfather spoke in 1868;

to Viviane Silverman who designed the sesquicentennial book and to Bethann Thornburgh who illustrated the cover;

to those individuals whose time and talents enhanced in various ways this book project: Ann Cook Cole, Eloise B. Waite, Joy Wicks, Sarah-Jane Gatley, Kim Kettle, Dorothy Baumle, Rhonda Lucas Donald, Mary Ellen Hughes, and Gerard Shelton;

to Martha Repman and Karen Lightner, Reference Librarians at The Free Library of Philadelphia;

(Continued on following page)

to Ebenezer Scrooge who we believe presented the Smoking Bishop recipe to our great-grandfather that Christmas of 1843;

to friends who contributed recipes over the years to our family;

I am profoundly grateful to Elizabeth and our families whose love makes our hearts able to contain the Spirit of Christmas so necessary for a happy life.

CHRISTMAS
with
DICKENS

Charles Dickens
Age 27

Kate Dickens
Age 24

A Christmas Carol, 1843

Devonshire Terrace
Twenty Fourth October 1843

My Dear Sir,

I am extremely sorry to find that my proposal puts you to any inconvenience . . . Accordingly I plunged headlong into a little scheme I had held in abeyance during the interval which had elapsed between my first letter and your answer; set an artist at work upon it; and put it wholly out of my own power to touch the Edinburgh subject until after Christmas is turned. For carrying out the notion I speak of, and being punctual with Chuzzlewit will occupy every moment of my waking time, up to the Christmas Holidays.

My Dear Sir/Faithfully Yours always

Charles Dickens

Devonshire Terrace/Wednesday morning

My Dear Miss Ely.

Forgive my not having answered your kind note; but I have been working from morning until night upon my little Christmas book; and have really had no time to think of anything but that.

I am much pleased by your sister's recollection of me, and if I can possibly get to the "Theatre" tonight (I have strong hopes of it for I am finishing now) — trust me, I will. For I have such a passion for anything in the shape of Private Theatricals — AH! You never saw me act! — as nobody but Mrs. Harris ever had.

We dine on Saturday — Kate begs me say, with her love to Mrs. Talfourd — at a Quarter before Seven.

Dear Miss Ely/Always Faithfully Yours

Charles Dickens

Miss Ely

5

Twenty First November 1843

My Dear George,

Many Thanks for the Almanack, in which you are prodigious.

I am afraid I may not be in the way tomorrow; and therefore write to you. For I am finishing a little Book for Christmas, and contemplate a Bolt, to do so in peace. As soon as I have done, I will let you know. And then I hope we shall take a glass of Grog together: for I have not seen you since I was grey.

Always Heartily Yours

Charles Dickens

George Cruikshank Esquire

61

Stave V.

The end of it.

Yes! and the bed post was his own.... The bed w[as]
Best and happiest of all the Time before
[the happiest]
"I will live in the Past, the Present, and the [future]...
.... The Spirit of all Three sh[all]... Jacob Marley....
...be praised for this! I say it on my knees, old...
...was so fluttered and so ... glowin[g]...
...moved scarce answer this call....
...been sobbing violently, in his conflict with the Spirit, and his face was...
...they are not torn down", cried Scrooge, folding...
..."they are not torn down. rings and all...
...shadows of the things that would have been...
...His hands were busy with his garments...
...putting them on upside down, tearing them, cosing th[em]...
...of extravagance.
"I don't know what to do!" cried Scrooge, laug[hing]...
I am as light as a feather, I am as happy...

Detail of Original Manuscript, *A Christmas Carol*

Nineteenth December 1843

My Dear MacKay.

Believe me that your pleasure in the *Carol*,
so earnestly and spontaneously expressed, gives
me real gratification of heart. It has delighted me
very much. I am sure you feel it; that your praise
is manly and generous; and well worth having.
Thank you heartily.

I was very much affected by the little Book
myself; in various ways, as I wrote it; and had an
interest in the idea, which made me reluctant to
lay it aside for a moment. . . .

I shall not forget your note, easily.

Always Faithfully Yours

Charles Dickens

Charles MacKay, Esquire

Facsimile Cover of First Edition
A Christmas Carol

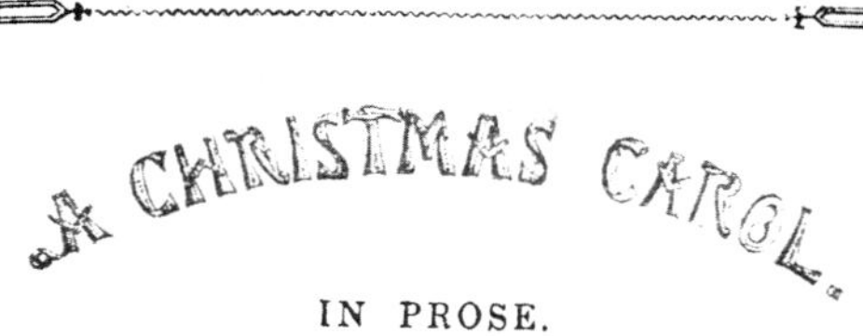

IN PROSE.

BEING

A Ghost Story of Christmas.

BY

CHARLES DICKENS

WITH ILLUSTRATIONS BY JOHN LEECH.

LONDON:
CHAPMAN & HALL, 186, STRAND.

Facsimile Title Page of First Edition
A Christmas Carol

Preface

I have endeavoured in this Ghostly little
book, to raise the Ghost of an Idea, which
shall not put my readers out of humour
with themselves, with each other, with the
season, or with me. May it haunt their house
pleasantly, and no one wish to lay it.

Their faithful Friend and Servant,

C.D.

December 1843

Preface of First Edition
A Christmas Carol

Devonshire Terrace/Friday Decr. 22nd 1843

My Dear Harness,

I have run short of copies of the *Carol*, owing to the demand, or I would have sent you this before.

I forget your pretty niece's Christian name. When you have read the little book, send it me back with that information; and I will write the same on the title page.

Faithfully yours

Charles Dickens

Devonshire Terrace
Twenty-seventh December, 1843

My dear Mitton,

You will be glad to hear that I had a note from Chapman and Hall on the twenty-fourth to say that the *Carol* was then in its Sixth Thousand; and that as the orders were coming in fast from town and country, it would soon be necessary to reprint. I am very glad you saw the children the other day, and made them so happy. I have much to say in reference to your note of last Friday, but cannot say it better perhaps than when France draws nearer to us. I shall see you within a day or two.

Ever faithfully

Charles Dickens

*"There was indeed nobody that had not
some interest in the message of the
Christmas Carol. It told the selfish man to rid
himself of selfishness; the just
man to make himself generous; and the good-
natured man to enlarge the sphere
of his good nature. Its cheery voice of faith and
hope, ringing from one end of the island
to the other, carried pleasant warning alike to all,
that if the duties of Christmas
were wanting, no good could come of its outward
observances; that it must shine
upon the hearth and warm it, and
into the sorrowful heart and comfort it; that it must
be kindness, benevolence, charity,
mercy, and forebearance, or its plum pudding
would turn to stone and its roast beef
be indigestible . . . ."*

The Life of Charles Dickens

Charles Dickens Reading
March l9th, l870

Guide to

A *Christmas Carol* Evening

*C*hristmas Carol dinners have been
held both in England and America, both in
domestic surroundings and in banquet rooms.
From our own experience, we offer this
Dickens "recipe" for a warm, memorable
evening. Adapt it to your setting among family,
friends, church groups, club members, or
business associates.

Christmas Carol Host or Hostess

This person acts as master of ceremonies.
He or she oversees the evening, moves it
forward on a positive note, and keeps it under
control. For the sake of brevity, we will refer to
"Host."

Provide the Host with *Christmas with
Dickens* as his programme script. His responsi-
bility is to:
    ❄ Conduct the evening
    ❄ Introduce the *Christmas Carol* Reader
    ❄ Call up the meal courses from the

kitchen
* ❄ Direct the dimming and raising of the lights
* ❄ Give the Grace
* ❄ Make the Toast
* ❄ Announce the Game and read the instructions (optional)
* ❄ Round off the proceedings

Christmas Carol Reader

Select someone who is at home in the limelight — usually easy to find! This person should have a good speaking voice, perhaps even experience in amateur dramatics.

One Reader can carry the evening, or a Reader can be assigned to each of the five *Christmas Carol* staves. Provide the Reader with *"A Note to the Programme Reader"* as he prepares for the evening, and with *Christmas with Dickens* as his programme script.

Christmas Carol Cook

Either the Cook or another member of the kitchen staff should have steady hands, a smiling face, and enjoy being the center of attention.

Provide the Cook ahead of time with his cues to:

* Parade the turkey around the room, when called by the Host
* Parade the flaming Christmas Pudding in the same manner
* Appear with the kitchen staff and serving persons when called by the Host

Table Plan

Take infinite trouble with the table plan, so that everyone is seated happily with congenial neighbours. If there are disabled people, place them so that they can be easily served. Allow for some who may prefer, say, vegetarian dishes, so that they, too, can be served without disruption or delay.

Menu

Build your own menu either from our family recipes or your own favourites.

Miniature menus can be used as place cards, with each guest's name boldly displayed. They will add gaiety to the table and become treasured keepsakes. One of the guests may wish to design the menus, using *Christmas Carol* quotations. The quotations scattered throughout the book are ideal for this purpose.

Victorian Period Clothing

The Victorian years' fashion was rich with top hats and bonnets, waistcoats and muffs. In this spirit, the Host or Reader may wish to wear period clothing, such as that shown on page 73. A few guests may want to dress similarly.

Decorations

Use holly, mistletoe, and ivy in abundant proportions. In *A Christmas Carol*, The Ghost of Christmas Past "held a branch of fresh green holly in its hand." The Ghost of Christmas Present "on its head wore no other covering than a holly wreath."

Victorian Period Music

Throughout *A Christmas Carol*, there is music. Charles Dickens wrote: "Scrooge's niece played well upon the harp," and "In came a fiddler with a music book." He described men in a solitary lighthouse who "struck up a sturdy song that was like a Gale in itself." Consider background music during the meal courses, either instrumental or a small group singing Christmas carols.

~

Menu Courses

Aperitifs
Starters
~
Fish Course
Main Course
~
Pudding Course
Smoking Bishop
Desserts

A Christmas Carol Dinner

Apple Fizz — Christmas Cheer

~

Warm Mushroom Salad

~

Sherried Prawns

~

Roast Turkey — Boiled Ham
accompanied by
Potatoes — Roast Parsnips — Brussels Sprouts
with Chestnuts
Applesauce — Cranberry Jelly — Gravy

~

Christmas Pudding — Mince Pies — Fruit Jelly
accompanied by
Brandy Butter — Ice Cream

~

Smoking Bishop

~

Stilton Cheese — Celery — Crisp Crackers
Sweetmeats — Roasted Chestnuts

~

Coffee

~

The Script for
the Programme Host

Time: Excerpts from *A Christmas Carol* have been edited for reading aloud. One excerpt — stave — precedes each meal course. The reading and speaking time for the evening's programme is a total of twenty-eight minutes.

Provide the Reader with "A Note to the Programme Reader" as he prepares for the evening, and *Christmas with Dickens* as his programme script.

The Host welcomes the guests as they assemble.

Aperitifs are served (pages 32 - 35).

The Host determines the time and announces: "Dinner is served!" He then leads the guests to the tables. When all are seated and settled, the Host reads the Introduction to the Evening (page 28). Allow two minutes.

The Host asks guests to bow their heads for the Dickensian Grace. Host reads the Grace (page 31).

The Host introduces the Reader in a hearty way, concluding with the words: "Stave One — Marley's Ghost." Allow one minute.

The Reader reads Stave One (pages 37 - 40). Allow four minutes.

Starters are served (pages 41 - 47).

The Host calls on the Reader to continue the evening's programme by announcing: "Stave Two — The First of the Three Spirits."

The Reader reads Stave Two (pages 49 - 56). Allow seven minutes.

The Fish Course is served (pages 57 - 69).

The Host calls on the Reader to continue: "Stave Three — The Second of the Three Spirits."

The Reader reads Stave Three (pages 71 - 78). Allow five minutes.

The Host calls on the Cook:
"Now Presenting the Turkey!"
The Cook parades the turkey around the room.

The Main Course is served (pages 79 - 93).

The Host calls on the Reader to continue:
"Stave Four — The Last of the Three Spirits."

The Reader reads Stave Four (pages 95 - 98). Allow three minutes.

The Host waits for the Reader's conclusion as his cue: ". . . and dwindle down into a bedpost." He then signals a designee to dim the lights or does it himself.

The Host calls on the Cook:
"Now Presenting the Christmas Pudding!"
The Cook parades the flaming Christmas Pudding around the room.

The Pudding Course is served (pages 99 - 105).

The Host calls on the Reader to continue:
"Stave Five — The End of It."

The Reader reads Stave Five (pages 106 -
113). Approaching the end, he should empha-
size these words: ". . . and we will discuss
your affairs this very afternoon, over a
Christmas bowl of smoking bishop, Bob."
The Reader then stops. (Allow four minutes).

After-Dinner Drinks are served (pages 114 - 125).

The Host signals for the lights to be raised.
He then calls the Cook, kitchen staff, waiters,
and waitresses into the room.

The Reader reads the final two paragraphs of
Stave Five (page 113). Allow one minute.

The Host expresses gratitude to the Reader,
the Cook, the kitchen staff, serving persons,
and especially to the guests. The Host announces: "May I propose this toast. Will

everyone lift a glass. In the spirit of Charles Dickens and Tiny Tim, God Bless Us, Every One!"

Dessert is served, followed by coffee (pages 126 - 131).

Games (optional)

Charles Dickens, his family and friends, enjoyed playing party games. **The Host** determines whether time allows and guests are in the mood for a game. If he suggests one, either he or a designated person should read aloud the game instructions (pages 132 - 141).

Epilogue

After such an orderly programme, we advise **the Host** to conclude with a spirited — very short — Epilogue. Allow one minute.

The Host says: "May Scrooge's words go with us this evening: 'I will honour Christmas in my heart, and try to keep it all the year. I will live in the Past, the Present, and the Future.'

"And from the Dickens family in England comes this special New Year's wish:

'May your New Year be a happy one:
Happy to many more whose happiness
depends on you;
God bless you, every one.
Good night.' "

The Host reads this aloud to the assembled guests. Time: two minutes.

Introduction to the Evening

A Christmas Carol was Charles Dickens' favorite story. He wrote it in 1843, because he cared about the poor and less fortunate. He loved people. He wanted everybody to be happy.

As Cedric Dickens, Charles Dickens' great-grandson, says, "He wrote rattling good stories to be read aloud, read to an audience of family and friends." With great emotion, he read aloud to his own family. Because he loved to act, Dickens soon began reading at public gatherings. At the first reading in 1853, *A Christmas Carol* took three hours to read. He set about condensing it — to one hour. In 1870, just weeks before his death, he gave a farewell reading. First on the programme, of course, was *A Christmas Carol*, followed by the *Trial from Pickwick*.

Just as the character Scrooge laughed and cried as he realized the true meaning of Christmas, Dickens' audiences laughed and cried as he read the delightful little story.

To commemorate the 150th anniversary of *A Christmas Carol*, Dickens' great-grandsons Cedric and David with David's wife Betty, created the idea for an evening built around the *Carol*. Their idea became a book called *Christmas with Dickens*. Our dinner and program this evening will evolve within this framework. Be assured that the readings have been condensed to twenty-five minutes! We will hear five short readings, interspersed with food and drink. And so, my friends, let us begin.

Allow your emotions to be expressed as Charles Dickens hoped, "in the most natural way." Imagine yourselves to be with a small group of friends around the fireside. See the candlelight and firelight casting shadows on the walls. Feel the warmth of those gathered with you.

Now let us bow our heads for this Dickensian prayer.

Dickensian Grace

In Fellowship assembled here
We thank thee, Lord, for food and cheer
And through our Saviour, thy dear Son,
We pray, "God bless us, every one."

This prayer was discovered by Alan S. Watts,
President of the Dickens Fellowship,
during research for his book *Dickens at Gad's Hill*.
You may prefer to use a family Grace,
a customary or otherwise favourite one instead.

Aperitifs

*"Wonderful party,
wonderful games, wonderful unanimity,
won-der-ful happiness!"*

A Christmas Carol

Apple Fizz

lump of cane sugar
Angostura bitters
teaspoon of fresh lime juice
apple juice, unsweetened
dry sparkling wine, good quality, chilled
  very cold
Calvados

1. Soak lump of cane sugar in Angostura bitters in a wine glass.
2. Add fresh lime juice.
3. Add a quarter-full glass of apple juice.
4. Add sparkling wine.
5. Float a few drops of Calvados on top.

Buck's Fizz

orange juice, freshly squeezed, strained, and chilled
dry champagne, chilled

1. Pour a quarter-full glass of orange juice.
2. Top up with champagne.

Christmas Cheer

lump of brown cane sugar
tablespoon of fresh lime juice
teaspoon of tinned lychee juice
apple juice
non-alcoholic drink
lychee
cherry
lemon rind, thinly peeled

1. Soak brown sugar in lime juice in a large wine glass.
2. Add lychee juice.
3. Add apple juice to half full.
4. Top up with a fizzy non-alcoholic drink of your choice.
5. Decorate with half a lychee and a cherry on a cocktail stick.
6. Add twist of lemon.

*Bob Cratchit in Scrooge's
Counting-House*

Stave One

Marley's Ghost

nce upon a time — of all the good days in the year, on Christmas Eve — Old Scrooge sat busy in his counting-house. It was cold, bleak, biting weather. Old Marley had died seven Christmas Eves ago. Yet Scrooge, his partner, his sole friend, and mourner, still was a tight-fisted hand at the grindstone. He was a squeezing, wrenching, grasping, scraping, clutching, covetous old sinner! Hard and sharp as flint, secret and self-contained, and solitary as an oyster. The cold within him froze his old features, nipped his pointed nose, made his eyes red, and his thin lips blue.

In the dismal little cell beyond, Scrooge's clerk, Bob Cratchit, tried to warm himself at a candle.

"A merry Christmas!" Scrooge's

nephew called out as he entered.

"Bah!" said Scrooge. "Humbug! Every idiot who goes about with 'Merry Christmas' on his lips, should be boiled with his own pudding, and buried with a stake of holly through his heart."

"But uncle," Fred pleaded. "I have always thought of Christmas as a good time: a forgiving, charitable, pleasant time: the only time I know of when men and women seem to open their shut-up hearts freely."

"Bah! Humbug!" Scrooge replied. "Good afternoon!"

That evening Scrooge sat alone in his dreary room at home. He heard a clanking noise, then a booming sound! Marley's Ghost approached him, dragging a long chain. The chain, wound about his middle, was made of cash-boxes, ledgers and heavy steel purses.

Scrooge trembled. "Why do you trouble me?"

"It is required of every man," the Ghost said, "that the spirit within him should walk

Marley's Ghost

Marley's Ghost Visits Scrooge

abroad among his fellow men, and travel far and wide. If that spirit goes not forth in life, it is condemned after death to wander through the world, to witness what it might have shared on Earth and turned to happiness—oh, woe is me!"

Scrooge shivered. "Speak comfort to me, Marley."

"I have none to give. You have yet a chance of escaping my fate. You will be haunted by Three Spirits."

"I—I think I'd rather not," said Scrooge.

"Without their visits," the Ghost said, "you cannot hope to shun the path I tread. Expect the first tomorrow, when the bell tolls one."

The Ghost began walking backward and floated out upon the bleak, dark night.

Old Scrooge tried to say "Humbug" but went straight to bed, without undressing. ❄

Starters

"... there is nothing in the world so irresistibly contagious as laughter and good-humour."

A Christmas Carol

Refer to Glossary and Conversion Table
for American word meanings and measurements.

Leek and Potato Soup

pound of leeks
3/4 pound of potatoes
1/2 ounce of butter
pint of stock or water
1/2 pint of milk
salt and pepper

1. Sweat leeks and potatoes in butter for approximately ten minutes, shaking the pan from time to time.
2. Boil stock or water, and add to pan of vegetables.
3. Simmer until soft.
4. Push through sieve or blend.
5. Add milk and seasonings to taste.
6. Heat to serve.

Yield: 4 to 5 servings

Warm Mushroom Salad

2 red peppers
32 button mushrooms

1. Place peppers under hot grill until charred all round.
2. Peel, remove seeds, and slice or dice.
3. Keep warm.
4. Sauté mushrooms gently in butter for about three minutes.
5. Keep warm.

Dressing

juice of one orange and a little grated rind
3 tablespoons of runny honey
tablespoon of vegetable oil
heaped teaspoon of dried tarragon
salt and pepper to taste

(Continued on following page)

1. Place all the ingredients in a screw-
   topped jar, cover, and shake well.
2. Prepare in advance to let the tarragon
   soften and release its flavour.

lettuce
sesame seeds

1. Arrange torn leaves of lettuce on serving
   plate.
2. Spoon on the cooked mushrooms, and
   arrange the red pepper round the edge.
3. Spoon dressing over.
4. Dust with sesame seeds.

Serve at once.

Yield: 4 servings

Fruit and Mint Vinaigrette

2 dessert apples, unpeeled
2 pears, unpeeled
juice of half a lemon
4 ounces of grapes
2 oranges
tablespoon of fresh chopped mint

1. Core and dice apples and pears.
2. Place in bowl, and pour lemon juice over.
3. Halve and remove seeds from grapes.
4. Peel oranges, and cut into chunks.
5. Add grapes and oranges to bowl with mint.
6. Stir well.
7. Cover with clingfilm, and leave in fridge for two to three hours.

(Continued on following page)

Dressing

3 tablespoons of wine vinegar
level teaspoon of salt
6 tablespoons of olive oil
4 tablespoons of double cream
6 sprigs of fresh mint

1. Place vinegar and salt in bowl, and leave
   for a few minutes for salt to dissolve.
2. Add olive oil.
3. Whisk well to blend.
4. Stir in double cream.

When ready to serve, divide fruit among
six dishes or glasses. Pour dressing over,
and garnish with sprig of mint.

Yield: 6 servings

Other Starters

Avocado

Canteloupe

Grapefruit

Paté

A Boy Intent upon His Reading

Stave Two

The First of the Three Spirits

Scrooge awoke as the church chimes tolled one — a deep, dull, hollow, melancholy One. Light flashed in the room, and Scrooge found himself face to face with a strange figure — like an old man diminished to a child's proportions. It held a branch of fresh green holly in its hand.

"Are you the spirit, sir?" asked Scrooge.

"I am. I am the Ghost of Christmas Past."

"Long past?" inquired Scrooge.

"No. Your past. Rise and walk with me. We will see the shadows of things that have been."

Together, they passed through the wall, into the country to a school. Inside, at a desk, a boy was intent upon his reading. Suddenly, a man in exotic clothing stood outside the school window.

"Why, it's dear old honest Ali Baba!" Scrooge exclaimed. "One Christmas time, when yonder solitary child was left here all alone, he did come, for the first time, just like that."

To hear Scrooge in a most extraordinary voice between laughing and crying would have been a surprise to his business friends.

The Ghost and Scrooge then left the school behind and went to a city where it was Christmas time again.

At a certain warehouse door, the Ghost stopped, and asked Scrooge if he knew it.

"Know it!" said Scrooge. "I was apprenticed here."

They went in, and at the sight of an old gentleman sitting behind a high desk, Scrooge cried in excitement:

"Why, it's old Fezziwig! Bless his heart; it's Fezziwig alive again!"

Old Fezziwig laid down his pen and called out: "Yo ho there! Ebenezer! Dick!"

Scrooge's former self, now a young man,

*A Fiddler
Tuned Like Fifty
Stomach-Aches*

came briskly in, accompanied by his fellow -
'prentice.

"Dick Wilkins, to be sure," said Scrooge
to the Ghost. "Bless me, yes. There he is."

"Yo ho, my boys!" said Fezziwig. "No
more work tonight! Christmas Eve, Dick.

Christmas, Ebenezer! Let's have the shutters up. Clear away, my lads, and let's have lots of room here!"

It was done in a minute. They made the warehouse as snug and bright a ballroom as you would desire to see upon a winter's night.

In came a fiddler and went up to the lofty desk, and made an orchestra of it, and tuned like fifty stomach-aches. In came Mrs. Fezziwig, one vast substantial smile. In came the three Miss Fezziwigs, beaming and lovable. In came the six young followers whose hearts they broke. In came all the young men and women employed in the business. Away they all went, twenty couples at once, down the middle and up again, round and round. Old Fezziwig clapped his hands and cried out, "Well done!"

There were more dances, and there were forfeits, and more dances, and there was cake, and there was a great piece of Cold Roast, and there were mince-pies, and plenty of beer.

During the whole of this time, Scrooge

The First of the Three Spirits

Mr. Fezziwig's Ball

remembered everything. He enjoyed every-thing, and underwent the strangest agitation.

"The happiness Fezziwig gives is quite as great as if it cost a fortune," Scrooge said and stopped.

"What's the matter?" asked the Ghost.

"Nothing particular," said Scrooge. "I should like to be able to say a word to my clerk just now. That's all."

Scrooge and the Ghost again stood side by side in the open air.

Now Scrooge saw himself, older, a man in the prime of life. He sat by the side of a fair young girl in whose eyes there were tears.

"Another idol has displaced me," she said softly.

"What idol has displaced you?" he asked.

"A golden one," she replied. "I have seen your nobler aspirations fall off one by one."

"I am not changed toward you," the younger Scrooge said.

"You are changed, and I release you, with a full heart, for the love of him you once were.

May you be happy in the life you have chosen!"

"Spirit! Show me no more!" cried Scrooge.

"One shadow more!" the Ghost exclaimed.

They were in another place: a room full of comfort, family laughter, tumultuous noise, with more children than Scrooge could count. The children shouted with delight at every Christmas package they received.

Near to the fire sat a beautiful young girl, so like the last that Scrooge believed it was the same, until he saw *her*, now a comely matron, sitting opposite her daughter.

And when he thought that such another creature might have called him father, and been a spring-time in the winter of his life, his sight grew very dim indeed.

By degrees, the children went to bed.

The husband turned to his wife with a smile.

"I saw an old friend of yours this afternoon."

"Who was it?" she asked.

"Mr. Scrooge. I passed his office window. His partner lies upon the point of death, and there he sat, alone. Quite alone in the world."

"Spirit!" said Scrooge in a broken voice. "I cannot bear it! Haunt me no longer!"

Scrooge was conscious of being exhausted, and further, of being in his own bedroom. He had barely time to reel into bed, before he sank into a heavy sleep.   ❄

Fish Course

*"... I have always thought of
Christmas time... as a good time:
a kind, forgiving, charitable
pleasant time...."*

A Christmas Carol

Sherried Prawns

pint of shelled prawns
3 ounces of butter
teaspoon of flour
1/2 cup of cream
2 tablespoons of sherry
egg yolk
teaspoon of lemon juice

1. Cook prawns gently for a few minutes in two-thirds of the butter.
2. Melt the rest of the butter, add flour and cream.
3. Cook gently. When it thickens, add prawns, sherry, and egg yolk. Be very careful that the egg yolk does not boil.
4. Add lemon juice. Stir well.

Serve with sippets of dry, thin toast.

Yield: 4 servings

Smoked Fish Puffs

puff pastry
small onion, chopped
clove of garlic, chopped
2 tomatoes, skinned and chopped
butter
pound of smoked haddock or cod
grated cheese, optional
black pepper

1. Line individual dishes with puff pastry, allowing surplus to overhang edges.
2. Sauté onion, garlic and tomatoes in butter until soft.
3. Add flaked, cooked, smoked fish and, if desired, grated cheese.
4. Season with pepper.
5. Spoon into pastry-lined dishes, and fold edges over.

(Continued on following page)

6. Bake in hot oven for about twenty
minutes.

Yield: 4 servings

Salmon Roulade

ounce of fresh white bread crumbs
3 ounces of Cheddar cheese, grated
2 eggs, size 3, separated
1/2 carton of soured cream ❄
1/4 level teaspoon of salt
pinch of cayenne pepper
tablespoon of warm water

1. Line a Swiss roll tin with greaseproof paper, leaving approximately two inches overhanging at each end. Brush with oil.
2. Set oven to fairly hot.
3. Mix the bread crumbs and cheese together.
4. Mix in the egg yolks, soured cream and seasonings.
5. Stir in the warm water.
6. Whisk egg whites until stiff, and fold

(Continued on following page)

into cheese mixture.

7. Spread mixture evenly in tin, and bake toward top of oven for fifteen minutes.
8. Remove from oven.
9. Wring out a clean tea towel with cold water, and lay over the roulade.
10. When cold, turn out onto a large sheet of greaseproof paper.
11. Remove lining paper.

Filling

8 ounces of smoked salmon trimmings or a 7 1/2-ounce tin of salmon
tomato
1/2 carton of soured cream ❊
rind of 1/2 lemon, finely grated
tablespoon of lemon juice
tablespoon of snipped chives
1/4 teaspoon of salt
pinch of pepper
lemon segments

1. Chop the smoked salmon trimmings finely. If using a tin of salmon, remove skin and bones, then flake the fish.
2. Remove skin and seeds from tomato, and chop.
3. Mix salmon with soured cream, lemon rind and juice, tomato, chives, and seasoning.
4. Spread mixture over roulade.
5. Roll up like a Swiss roll, using the greaseproof paper to help.
6. Chill for at least one hour.

Serve with lemon segments.

Yield: 4 to 6 servings

❊ NOTE: For American conversion, measure
1/8 pint of soured cream in **Roulade**
and **1/8 pint of soured cream** in **Filling**.

Smoked Salmon Mousse

pound of smoked salmon pieces
12 fluid ounces of water
1/2 pint of double cream
3 eggs, separated
3/4 tablespoon of gelatine
paprika
salt
lemon juice
prawns
parsley sprigs
lemon wedges

1. Chop smoked salmon into small pieces.
2. Keeping some for decoration, blend smooth using nearly all the water.
3. Warm cream over a pan of hot water.
4. Beat into the egg yolks thoroughly.
5. Dissolve gelatine in water, and add to the mixture, with paprika, a little salt, and lemon juice to taste.

6. Allow the mixture to get quite cold, then stir in blended salmon.
7. Beat egg whites until stiff, and carefully fold them in.
8. Pour into individual dishes or bowls.
9. Put in fridge until set.

Before serving, turn out on plates. Decorate with pieces of smoked salmon, and surround with prawns, parsley sprigs and lemon wedges.

Yield: 4 to 6 servings

Moules Marinière

5 pints of mussels   cold water
1/2 pint of dry white wine   salt
4 shallots   oatmeal
butter
4 tablespoons of parsley and thyme,
    finely chopped
bay leaf
flour
2 pints of chicken stock
1/2 pint of single cream
parsley
black pepper

1. Twelve hours before cooking, scrub the mussels. Discard those that are broken or open.
2. Put into a pail of cold water with a handful of salt and oatmeal.
3. Throughout preparation time, use several changes of fresh water, scrub,

scrape, and again discard any open mussels.

4. With the final change of water, remove the little tuft of hair on the middle of the hinge side - its beard.
5. Place a bowl in the oven with white wine in it. Heat. Keep in oven until needed.
6. Sauté the finely chopped shallots in a spoonful of butter until transparent.
7. Add the white wine, chopped parsley and thyme, and the bay leaf.
8. Season to taste with black pepper.
9. Add mussels and cook on a hot flame, shaking constantly.
10. Strain the liquid in which the mussels have been cooked.
11. As shells open, take the hot bowl with wine from the oven. Remove one half of each shell and put the other, containing the mussel, into the bowl.

(Continued on following page)

12. In a separate saucepan, melt two tablespoons of butter over a low flame.
13. Add flour, stir well, and cook for two to three minutes without browning.
14. Add chicken stock, slowly stirring over heat.
15. Add cream and one-half of the mussels' liquid.
16. Pour over the mussels in the bowl.
17. Sprinkle with parsley.

Serve from the bowl into hot soup plates.

Yield: 4 servings

Other Fish Course Suggestions

Crab

Oysters

Scallops

Smoked Salmon

Trout

Whitebait

The Ghost of Christmas Present

Stave Three

The Second of the Three Spirits

When the bell struck one, Scrooge sat up in bed to get his thoughts together. A strange voice called him by name. He got up softly and shuffled in his slippers to the door.

"Come in!" said the spirit. "I am the Ghost of Christmas Present."

The room was Scrooge's own room, but it had undergone a surprising transformation. The walls and ceiling were hung with living green — holly, mistletoe and ivy. Heaped up on the floor to form a kind of throne, were turkeys, geese, poultry, mince-pies, plum-puddings, red-hot chestnuts, and juicy oranges. Upon this couch, there sat a jolly Giant, glorious to see; who bore a glowing torch, in shape like Plenty's horn, and held it up, high up, to shed its light on Scrooge.

The Spirit was clothed in a deep green

robe, bordered with white fur. On its head it wore a holly wreath. Its dark curls were free, as free as its cheery voice and its joyful air.

"Spirit," Scrooge said, "last night I learnt a lesson which is working now. Tonight, if you have aught to teach me, let me profit by it."

They went straight to Bob Cratchit's dwelling which the Spirit blessed with the sprinkling of his torch.

In came Bob, the father, in his thread-bare clothes with Tiny Tim upon his shoulder. Alas for Tiny Tim, he bore a little crutch, and had his limbs supported by an iron frame! The two younger Cratchits escorted him off to where the pudding cooked.

"Coming home," Bob told his wife, "Tim said he hoped the people saw him in the church, because he was a cripple, and it might be pleasant to them to remember on Christmas Day, who made lame beggars walk and blind men see."

Scrooge watched the Cratchits bustle about their modest kitchen in the flushed

Bob with Tiny Tim upon His Shoulder

*The Cratchits Welcome Home Bob
and Tiny Tim*

anticipation of the Christmas feast to come. You might have thought a goose the rarest of all birds. Mrs. Cratchit made the gravy hissing hot; Master Peter plunged a fork into the saucepan of potatoes; Miss Belinda sweetened up the applesauce; Martha dusted the hot plates; Bob took Tiny Tim beside him in a tiny corner at the table; the two young Cratchits crammed spoons into their mouths, lest they should shriek for goose before their turn came to be helped.

At last the dishes were set on, and Grace was said.

Then a murmur of delight arose. There never was such a goose! Eked out by the applesauce and mashed potatoes, it was a sufficient dinner for the whole family.

Mrs. Cratchit left the room alone to bring in the pudding. It was like a speckled cannonball, so hard and firm, blazing in ignited brandy, with Christmas holly stuck into the top.

Oh, a wonderful pudding! Bob Cratchit

said, and calmly too, that he regarded it as the greatest success achieved by Mrs. Cratchit since their marriage. Mrs. Cratchit said that now the weight was off her mind, she would confess she had had her doubts about the quantity of flour.

At last the dinner was all done. The Cratchit family drew round the hearth, Bob served the hot stuff from a jug, and then proposed: "A Merry Christmas to us all, my dears. God bless us!"

"God bless us every one," said Tiny Tim.

"Spirit," said Scrooge, "tell me if Tiny Tim will live."

"I see a vacant seat," replied the Ghost, "and a crutch without an owner. If these shadows remain unaltered by the Future, the child will die."

"Oh, no, kind Spirit! Say he will be spared."

Without a word of warning from the Ghost, they sped to a room where Scrooge heard a hearty laugh. He recognized it as his own nephew's. There is nothing in the world so irresistibly contagious as laughter and good-humour!

"He said that Christmas was a humbug!" Scrooge's nephew told his wife and their assembled friends.

"You always tell me he is very rich, Fred," hinted Scrooge's niece.

"His wealth is of no use to him," said Scrooge's nephew. "He may rail at Christmas till he dies, but I defy him, by going there, year after year, and saying 'Uncle Scrooge, how are you?' If it only puts him in the vein to leave his poor clerk fifty pounds, *that's* something."

After tea, they had some music, and then they played at forfeits; for it is good to be children sometimes, and never better than at Christmas, when its mighty Founder was a child himself.

They played a game of Blindman's Buff, and after that a game called How, When, and Where. Young and old, they all played, and so did Scrooge. He sometimes came out with the guess quite loud, and very often guessed quite right. But the whole scene passed off in the breath of the last word spoken. The bell struck twelve. Scrooge looked about him for the Ghost and saw it not.

Instead he beheld a solemn Phantom, draped and hooded, coming, like a mist along the ground, towards him.   ❄

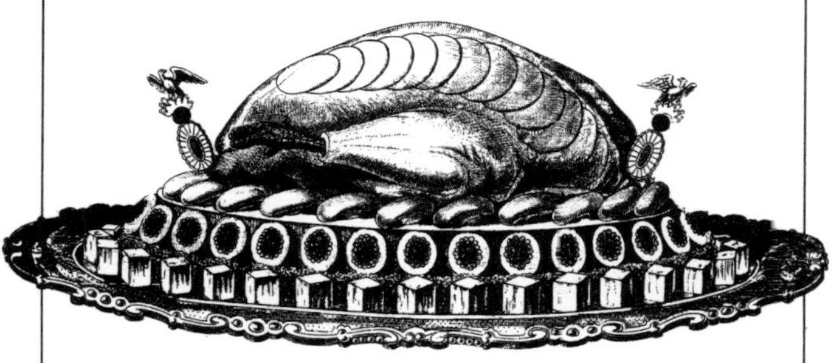

*"An intelligent boy!" said Scrooge.
"A remarkable boy!
Do you know whether they've sold the
prize Turkey that was hanging up there?
Not the little prize Turkey:
the big one?"*

*"What, the one as big as me?"
returned the boy.*

A Christmas Carol

Main Course

Many people have their own ways to prepare holiday turkey and goose. We suggest these recipes, along with our favourite recipes for turkey stuffings. We, also, include directions for curing your own ham.

Roast Turkey

10 ounces of mushroom caps
10-pound turkey
rind of two large lemons, thinly peeled
six-inch sprig of rosemary
pound of unsalted pork fat

1. Scald the mushrooms.
2. Fill the turkey with the lemon rind, potatoes and rosemary. (These impart fragrance and flavour and moisten the inside of the turkey.)

3. Loosen the skin of the upper part of the turkey until you can slide the mushrooms, caps up, under the skin. (This further enhances the flavour.)
4. Slice thinly some of the pork fat, and cover the breast with it.
5. Remove rind, and chop the remaining fat roughly. Put in bottom of the baking tin.
6. Set the bird in the baking tin, and cover with foil.
7. Cook in hot oven for thirty minutes, then reduce heat to moderate.
8. Allow fifteen minutes per pound, and then test with a steel knitting needle. If the juices oozing are pink, cook another fifteen minutes, and test again. When juices are only faintly pink, remove potatoes, lemon peel, and rosemary.

Yield: 10 to 15 servings

Chestnut Stuffing

ounce of butter
large onion, chopped
2 sticks of celery, thinly sliced
4 ounces of mushrooms, sliced
15-ounce can of chestnut puree
4 ounces of bread crumbs
egg
tablespoon of brandy
salt and pepper

1. Heat the butter, and add onion and celery.
2. Cook until transparent.
3. Add the mushrooms, and sauté for a few minutes.
4. Remove from heat, add chestnut puree and bread crumbs.
5. Leave to cool.
6. Beat in the egg, brandy, and plenty of seasoning.

Apricot Stuffing ❈

ounce of butter
onion, chopped
4 tablespoons of bread crumbs
salt and pepper
1/2 teaspoon of parsley, chopped
1/2 teaspoon of sage, chopped
1 to 2 tablespoons of milk
1/2 cup of dried apricots, chopped

1. Gently sauté the onion in butter.
2. Add bread crumbs, salt, pepper and herbs.
3. Mix with milk.
4. Add apricots.

❈ NOTE: For American conversion, **double** the recipe to fill the crop (neck) end of a turkey. **Quadruple** the recipe to fill a turkey's body.

Roast Goose

10-pound young goose

Pour boiling water over and in the bird the night before, and dry well. Hang the bird by the neck in an airy place.

2 1/2 teaspoons of honey
7 tablespoons of soya sauce
2 teaspoons of malt

1. Melt the honey with soya sauce and malt.
2. Rub the mixture into the bird's skin for about ten minutes to thoroughly coat it.

3. Cover the bottom of the oven with foil, and place on it a large baking tin containing water.
4. Pre-heat the oven to hot.
5. Fill the bird's entire body with stuffing.
6. Place the bird on a wire rack near the top.
7. Allow fifteen minutes per pound to cook. After thirty minutes, reduce heat to moderate. Try not to open the oven and peek.
8. Test with a steel knitting needle.

Stuffing

onion
8 potatoes
2 1/2 tablespoons of butter
egg yolk
teaspoon of marjoram, chopped, mixed with thyme

(Continued on following page)

salt and pepper

1. Parboil the onion and finely chop.
2. Boil potatoes, drain and thoroughly dry.
3. Mash potatoes.
4. Blend in butter, egg yolk and herbs.
5. Add salt, pepper and onion.

Yield: 8 servings

Ham

Curing

leg of pork, approximately 10 pounds
8 pints of water
1 1/2 pounds of coarse salt, preferably
*   sea salt*
2 ounces of salt petre
pound of dark brown sugar
2 ounces of Jamaica pepper, allspice
ounce of peppercorns
tablespoon of coriander seeds
8 juniper berries, crushed

1. Boil all the ingredients, except for the pork, for five minutes.
2. Leave to cool.
3. Strain into a deep, clean bucket, and completely immerse the joint in it.
4. Leave for ten to fourteen days.

(Continued on following page)

5. Remove joint from brine, and wash thoroughly.
6. Soak in fresh water for four hours.

Cooking

1. Place in cold water, and bring to a boil.
2. Simmer for thirty minutes to a pound.

Yield: 16 to 20 servings

Cabbage

2 ounces of butter
tablespoon of oil
onion, finely chopped
2 pounds of red cabbage, chopped
2 tablespoons of red wine vinegar
1/2 teaspoon of ground cloves
1/4 cup of white raisins
teaspoon of fine brown sugar
salt and pepper to taste

1. Melt butter and oil, and sauté the onion gently until transparent.
2. Add the other ingredients.
3. Put into a casserole, and cook slowly for at least an hour.

Cooking the day before and re-heating will enhance the flavour.

Yield: 6 to 7 servings

Roast Parsnips

4 parsnips, unpeeled
tablespoon of oil

1. Quarter the parsnips.
2. Brush with oil.
3. Roast round the meat.

Yield: 4 servings

———————

New Potatoes

*12 potatoes, approximately 1 1/2
    inches each*
salt
water
butter
mint, chopped

1. Remove potato skins.
2. Boil.

Serve in a hot dish, drenched with butter and
chopped mint.

Yield: 8 servings

An old gardener once told us that in his family the first new potatoes of the season to be dug were put in a tin with salt and buried in the garden. Part of his family's Christmas ritual was to find the tin, dig it up, and cook the potatoes for Christmas dinner. We adapt his custom by putting new potatoes in the deep freezer!

Other Vegetable Suggestions

Everybody has a favourite vegetable
to serve with Christmas dinner. Some of
our other favourites are Bubble
and Squeak (see page 145) and brussels
sprouts with chestnuts.

*Peter Cratchit Plunges
a Fork into the
Saucepan of Potatoes*

*The Ghost of Christmas Yet to Come
with Scrooge*

The Last of the Spirits

The Phantom was shrouded in a deep black garment, which concealed all but one outstretched hand.

"Am I in the presence of the Ghost of Christmas Yet To Come?" asked Scrooge.

The Spirit answered not, but pointed onward.

The city seemed to spring up around them. Merchants hurried up and down, and chinked the money in their pockets, and looked at their watches.

The Spirit stopped beside one little knot of businessmen and pointed to them.

"I only know he's dead," said a great fat man with a monstrous chin. "He died last night, I believe."

"I haven't heard what he's done with his money," another said. "He hasn't left it to me."

The Ghost conducted him through several streets. Scrooge looked here and there to find himself, but nowhere was he to be seen. They entered poor Bob Cratchit's house where it was quiet. Very quiet.

"Tiny Tim was very light to carry," Mrs. Cratchit told the children seated around the fire. "Your father loved him so, that it was no trouble."

She hurried out to meet her husband.

"My dear, I wish you could have gone with me," he said. "It would have done you good to see how green a place it is. But you'll see it often. My little, little child!" he cried.

He broke down all at once. He couldn't help it.

Mrs. Cratchit kissed him, his daughters kissed him, the two young Cratchits kissed him, and Peter and himself shook hands.

The Spirit stopped; its hand was pointed elsewhere.

Scrooge hastened to the window of his office, and looked in. It was an office still, but not his. The Phantom pointed as before.

A churchyard, overrun by grass and weeds. The Spirit stood among the graves, and pointed down to One.

Scrooge crept toward it, trembling as he went; and following the finger, read upon the stone of the neglected grave his own name, EBENEZER SCROOGE.

The finger pointed from the grave to him, and back again.

"Spirit!" he cried, "hear me! I am not the man I was. Assure me that I yet may change these shadows you have shown me, by an altered life!"

The Phantom's kind hand trembled.

"I will honour Christmas in my heart, and try to keep it all the year. I will live in the Past, the Present, and the Future. The Spirits of all Three shall strive within me. I will not shut out the lessons that they teach."

Holding up his hands in a last prayer to have his fate reversed, Scrooge saw the Phantom's hood shrink, collapse, and dwindle down into a bedpost.   ❄

*"Spirit of Tiny Tim,
thy childish essence
was from God!"*

A Christmas Carol

"In half a minute Mrs. Cratchit entered . . . with the pudding, like a speckled cannon-ball, so hard and firm, blazing in half of half-a-quartern of ignited brandy and bedight with Christmas holly stuck into the top."

A Christmas Carol

Christmas Pudding

pound of plain flour
pound of dark brown sugar
teaspoon of mixed spice
pound of bread crumbs
pound of suet, chopped
pound of sultanas
pound of currants
pound of seedless raisins
4 ounces of figs
4 ounces of prunes
1/2 pound of apples, grated
2 oranges grated, rind and juice
2 lemons grated, rind and juice
1/2 pound of almonds, chopped and peeled
6 eggs
pint of old ale
glass of brandy

Prepare the pudding with family and friends around, if possible. The love coming from their hearts through their arms into the wooden spoon will enhance the quality of the pudding! While stirring, each person makes his own secret wish.

1. Sift flour, sugar, and mixed spice in a
   bowl.
2. Stir in bread crumbs and chopped suet.
   Set the bowl aside.
3. Mix all the fruit, nuts, and grated rind in
   a second bowl.
4. Add to the first ingredients, and mix well.
5. Break the eggs into a bowl, and whisk
   eggs with orange and lemon juice, old
   ale and brandy.
6. Add to the dry ingredients, and mix well.

(Continued on following page)

7. Apply oil to inside of four two-pint pudding basins, and fill basins with pudding mixture.
8. Leave until the next day, and steam for eight hours. Make sure the water does not boil away.

Before serving, turn out on plates. Pour brandy on and ignite, as Mrs. Cratchit did in *A Christmas Carol*. At the table, serve individual portions.

*Mrs. Cratchit
with the Pudding*

Brandy Butter

3 ounces of unsalted butter
3 ounces of caster sugar
1 1/2 tablespoons of brandy
teaspoon of lemon juice

1. Beat the butter until creamy.
2. Add the sugar a little at a time until all is well incorporated.
3. Add the brandy gradually.
4. Add the lemon juice.
5. Chill for several hours before serving.

Brandy Butter is excellent with both Christmas Pudding and Mince Pies. If you like it as much as we do, double or treble the recipe.

Mince Pies

Each of you probably has his own favourite recipe with shortcrust or puff pastry, with big or small lids. Our recommendation relates to serving. We think it essential to stick a fork into the top of the mince pie, and dribble brandy through the fork! On individual pies, allow a teaspoon of brandy for each pie.

Other Suggestions

Fruit Jelly with Ice Cream

Some people — particularly children — may prefer this to pudding.

Bombe Alaska

Using your favourite recipe, pour brandy around and flame it in the same way as Christmas Pudding.

∼

Stave Five

The End of It

Yes! and the bedpost was his own. The bed was his own, the room was his own. Best and happiest of all, the time before him was his own, to

106

make amends in!

"I will live in the Past, the Present, and the Future!" Scrooge repeated, as he scrambled out of bed.

He was glowing with his good intentions, and his face was wet with tears.

"I am as light as a feather," cried Scrooge. "I am as happy as an angel, I am as merry as a schoolboy. A merry Christmas to everybody! A happy New Year to all the world!"

Running to the window, he opened it and put out his head. No fog, no mist: clear, bright Golden sunlight.

"What's today?" cried Scrooge, calling

downward to a boy in Sunday clothes.

"Today?" replied the boy. "Why, CHRIST-MAS DAY."

"It's Christmas Day!" said Scrooge to himself. "I haven't missed it. The Spirits have done it all in one night. They can do anything they like. Of course they can. Hallo, my fine fellow!"

"Hallo!" returned the boy.

"Do you know the Poulterer's, in the next street but one, at the corner?"

"I should hope I did," replied the lad.

"An intelligent boy!" said Scrooge. "Do you know whether they've sold the prize Turkey that was hanging up there? Not the little prize Turkey: the big one?"

"The one as big as me?" replied the boy. "It's hanging there now."

"Is it?" said Scrooge. "Go and buy it, and tell 'em to bring it here, that I may give them the direction where to take it. Come back with the man in less than five minutes, and I'll give you half-a-crown."

The End of It

Scrooge Buys the Prize Turkey

*Scrooge Goes
to Church*

"I'll send it to Bob Cratchit's!" whispered Scrooge, rubbing his hands and splitting with a laugh. "He shan't know who sends it. It's twice the size of Tiny Tim."

Shaving that morning was not an easy task; shaving requires attention, even when you don't dance while you're at it. He dressed himself "all in his best," and at last got out into the streets. Walking with his hands behind him, Scrooge regarded everyone with a delighted smile.

He went to church, and walked about the streets, and found that everything could yield him pleasure. In the afternoon, he turned his steps toward his nephew's house.

He passed the door a dozen times, before he had the courage to go up and knock.

"Why bless my soul!" cried Fred, "who's that?"

"It's your uncle Scrooge. I have come to dinner. Will you let me in, Fred?"

Let him in! It was a mercy he didn't shake his arm off. He was at home in five minutes. Wonderful party, wonderful games, wonderful unanimity, won-der-ful happiness!

But he was early at the office the next morning. If only he could catch Bob Cratchit coming late!

And he did it! Bob was a full eighteen minutes and a half behind his time.

"Hallo!" growled Scrooge. "What do you

Scrooge Arrives at His Nephew's Dinner

mean by coming here at this time of day?"

"It's only once a year, sir," pleaded Bob. "It shall not be repeated. I was making rather merry yesterday, sir."

"I am not going to stand this sort of thing any longer," said Scrooge, leaping from his stool, "and therefore I am about to raise your salary!"

Bob trembled.

"A merrier Christmas, Bob, my good

fellow, than I have given you, for many a year! I'll raise your salary, and endeavour to assist your struggling family, and we will discuss your affairs this very afternoon, over a Christmas bowl of smoking bishop, Bob!"

Scrooge was better than his word. He did it all, and infinitely more; and to Tiny Tim, who did NOT die, he was a second father. He became as good a friend, as good a master, and as good a man, as the good old city knew, or any other good old city, town, or borough, in the good old world. Some people laughed to see the alteration in him, but he let them laugh; for he was wise enough to know that nothing ever happened on this globe, for good, at which some people did not have their fill of laughter in the outset. His own heart laughed: and that was quite enough for him.

It was always said of him, that he knew how to keep Christmas well, if any man alive possessed the knowledge. May that be truly said of us, and all of us! And so, as Tiny Tim observed, **God Bless Us, Every One!**   ❄

After-Dinner Drinks

" . . . and we will discuss your affairs this very afternoon, over a Christmas bowl of smoking bishop, Bob!"

A Christmas Carol

Smoking Bishop

A Christmas Carol tells us that the reformed Scrooge offered Smoking Bishop to Bob Cratchit. This exquisite drink has become a tradition at our holiday parties.

If someone in your party has a bald head, watch him as the drink works — medicinally, of course. His pate will blush! It is an incredible fact that you can feel the temperature going up to the very top of your head.

Christmas Present

Smoking Bishop is best made with Seville oranges which are not imported into English shops until January. The first year we made it, we used the recipe that follows:

(Continued on following page)

5 sweet oranges, unpeeled
old-fashioned grapefruit, not pink,
   unpeeled
36 cloves
1/4 pound of sugar, more or less, to taste
2 bottles of strong red wine
bottle of ruby port

1. Wash the fruit and bake in a moderate oven until golden brown. Turn once.
2. Prick each piece of fruit with six cloves each, a messy business.
3. Place into a warmed earthenware or glass bowl.
4. Add the sugar and red wine — NOT the port.
5. Cover and leave for at least twelve hours in a warm place.
6. Squeeze the fruit into the wine and strain.
7. Add the bottle of port and heat. DO NOT BOIL.

8. Pour into clean hot wine bottles, and
   stand in simmering water.
   (We have found this the perfect way to
   keep the Smoking Bishop really hot and
   easy to serve.)

Serve in small, stem wine glasses half full.
Keep topping up, but never beyond the
half-way mark!

Yield: 15 to 20 servings

Christmas Yet to Come

Make this recipe of Smoking Bishop in January, and cork for the coming Christmas season's party.

6 Seville oranges, unpeeled
36 cloves
1/4 pound of sugar, more or less, to taste
2 bottles of red wine
orange brandy

1. Wash the fruit, and bake in a moderate oven until golden brown.
   Turn once.
2. Prick the fruit with six cloves each.
3. Place into a warmed earthenware or glass bowl.
4. Add the sugar and red wine.
5. Add a large tot of orange brandy, homemade, if possible.
6. Bottle and cork securely.

Eleven months later, the following December —

bottle of ruby port
bottle of water

Before serving, add the bottle of port and the bottle of water. You will have the perfect Smoking Bishop.

Yield: 20 to 25 servings

Orange Brandy

8 Seville oranges
4 large lemons
3 pounds of loaf sugar
gallon of good brandy

1. Peel the oranges and lemons very thinly.
2. Pound the sugar fine.
3. Combine oranges, lemons and sugar in a jar.
4. Add the brandy, and cover the jar tightly.
5. Stir every third day for three weeks.
6. Strain and bottle, sealing the corks with wax.

Orange Brandy, if made in early to mid-November, can be drunk for your Christmas Present party. However, it is best left for two years to be drunk at a Christmas Yet to Come party. This lets the full flavour come out.

Serve in liqueur glasses.

Yield: 45 to 50 servings

Shrub

Charles Dickens refers to this drink as "srub." We have given you this choice of recipes. If you make it at the same time as Orange Brandy, you can use the fruit from that recipe for Shrub.

Shrub I

2 lemons, peeled
1/2 pint of lemon juice
3/4 pint of orange juice
1/2 gallon of rum
2 pounds of loaf sugar
water

1. Slice lemon peel very thinly.
2. Combine lemon peel with the lemon juice, orange juice, and rum in a large covered jar.
3. Let it stand for two days.

4. Dissolve sugar in a large bowl of water.
5. Pour the sugar water over the juice and spirits mixture.
6. Remove the lemon peel.
7. Leave for twelve days before serving.

Serve in wine glasses.

Yield: 15 to 20 servings

Shrub II

1/2 pint of Seville orange juice, strained
2 pounds of crystal sugar
3 pints of rum or brandy

1. Chill the orange juice.
2. Dissolve sugar in orange juice.

(Continued on following page)

3. Blend with rum or brandy.
4. Strain through a jelly bag.
5. Bottle and cork.

Serve in cocktail glasses.

Yield: 15 to 20 servings

"The compound in the jug being tasted,
and considered perfect,
apples and oranges were put
upon the table, and a shovel-full of
chestnuts on the fire.
Then all the Crachit family drew
round the hearth . . . ."

A Christmas Carol

Dickens Inn Coffee

*coffee, black, hot, strong and sweetened
    to taste*
measure of Cointreau
measure of Tia Maria
dollop of whipped cream
touch of cinnamon

1. Pour coffee three-fourths full into a tapered stem glass.
2. Stir in Cointreau.
3. Mix Tia Maria, whipped cream and cinnamon in a cup, then spoon mixture on top of the coffee.

This delectable drink is served at the Dickens Inn, Philadelphia.

Desserts

Young Scrooge and His Sister
Enjoy Dainties

A Christmas Carol

Assorted Desserts

Stilton cheese —celery —crisp crackers

∿

shiny red apples — pears — satsumas
oranges — black and white grapes — bananas
arranged in a large decorative fruit bowl

∿

sweetmeats
shelled and sugared almonds — raisins
glacé fruits — dates — figs

∿

chocolates — rum truffles — peppermint
creams — Turkish delight

∿

stem ginger — Carlsbad plums

∿

roasted chestnuts — walnuts
assorted other nuts

∿

coffee

∿

Glacé Fruit

Years ago, a South African friend told us about his making glacé peaches and drying them in the sun. He sent us a box for Christmas which were delicious. We give you this recipe for making your own glacé fruit.

*peaches or pears — peeled and pitted or
    cored and quartered*
*pineapples — peeled, sliced, and cut into
    wedge-shaped pieces*
*apricots, fleshy plums, and greengages —
    pricked several times to the centre with
    a stainless steel fork*
sugar
glucose

1. Choose any well-flavoured fruit in
    season, not too ripe.

2. Cover the prepared fruit with boiling
   water and simmer gently until just
   tender, when tested with a fine skewer:
   ten to fifteen minutes for firm fruit;
   three to four minutes for tender fruit.
   DO NOT OVERCOOK.
3. Place the fruit in a bowl.
4. For each one pound of fruit, make a
   syrup, combining one-half pint of water
   in which the fruit was cooked with two
   ounces of sugar and four ounces of
   glucose. Stir until sugar and glucose are
   dissolved, then bring to a boil.
5. Pour the boiling syrup over the fruit,
   making sure liquid covers the fruit. If
   you need more syrup, prepare in the
   same proportions. Keep fruit below the
   surface with a saucer or plate. Leave for
   twenty-four hours.
6. Drain syrup into a saucepan. Add two
   ounces of sugar for each original one-

(Continued on following page)

half pint of water. Bring to a boil, and pour again over fruit in the bowl. Leave for twenty-four hours.

7. Repeat Step 6 each day for three days.

8. Add three ounces of sugar for each original one-half pint of water, heat and stir to dissolve in the saucepan. Add the drained fruit, boil for three or four minutes, then pour back into the bowl. Leave for forty-eight hours.

9. Repeat Step 8. When the resulting syrup cools, it should be of the consistency of fairly thick honey. Soak for four days. If the syrup is still thin when it cools, repeat Step 8 again, then soak for four more days.

10. Use a fork to remove the fruit from the syrup. Place on a wire cake rack over a plate for a few minutes to drain.

11. Put the rack in a very cool oven to dry. With an electric cooker, use residual heat; with a gas cooker, use the lowest possible setting. If residual heat is used,

drying may take two to three days. If heat is continuous, drying should take three to six hours. Turn the fruit with a fork, until it is no longer sticky to handle.

In the summer and with the right climate, the fruit should be dried in the sunshine for a few hours.

12. Pack fruit in boxes with waxed paper between layers. This will keep for many months.

Preparation time: 11 to 15 days

Games

A Game of Blindman's Buff

A Christmas Carol

After completing *A Christmas Carol*, Charles Dickens celebrated the Christmas of 1843 with zest and vigour. He wrote his American friend, Cornelius Melton: "Such dinings, such dancings, such conjurings, such blindman's buffings, such theatre-goings, never took place in these parts before."

Since he enjoyed party games, Dickens wrote about them in *A Christmas Carol*. Guests at Mr. Fezziwig's Ball played Forfeits. Scrooge's nephew's dinner party guests played Yes and No and a riotous game of Blindman's Buff.

Our family continues to enjoy after-dinner games in the Dickens Christmas tradition.

Join our fun!

Forfeits

One person at a table is appointed the Judge. Each other person gives the Judge a personal belonging, such as tie, scarf, key, or handkerchief.

When these belongings are collected, a second person selects one object and holds it up behind the Judge, asking, "What forfeit has to be performed to redeem this belonging?"

The Judge pronounces the forfeit. The owner of the object must then perform the task set to reclaim his belonging.

Each object in turn is held up for a forfeit.

"After a while they played
at forfeits; for it is good to be children
sometimes, and never better than
at Christmas, when its mighty Founder
was a child himself."

A Christmas Carol

Suggested Forfeits

❅ Kiss your shadow on the wall.

❅ Leave the room with two legs and come in with six.
(This seemingly impossible task is quite simple. All the player has to do is go out of the room and return with a chair.)

❅ Sing a song.

❅ Name five animals with names beginning with a 'D'.

❅ Make at least three people laugh.

❅ Recite a poem or nursery rhyme and count the words as you go.

❅ Yawn until you can make someone else yawn.

❅ Put one hand where the other cannot touch it.
(The player accomplishes this by grasping the right elbow with the

(Continued on following page)

left hand or vice versa.)
❋ Name Scrooge's girlfriend, his sister or
his nephew.
❋ Kiss a book inside and out without
opening it.
(The player takes the book he has been
given with him out of the room.
He kisses the book, comes back
into the room, kisses it again,
and places it on the table.)

Blindman's Buff

One player is chosen to be the blindman. He is blindfolded with a handkerchief tied over his eyes and turned round two or three times to make detection more difficult. He attempts to catch any other player.

The other players tap him on the shoulder or pull at his sleeve to distract him. When he catches someone, he must guess the person's identity. If the person is identified, he then becomes the blindman, and the game begins again.

"There was first a game at blindman's buff.
Of course there was . . . the way
he went after that plump sister in the lace
tucker, was an outrage on the
credulity of human nature. Knocking down

(Continued on following page)

*the fire-irons, tumbling over
the chairs, bumping against the piano,
smothering himself among
the curtains, wherever she went,
there went he . . . ."*

A Christmas Carol

La-Di-Da

Our family plays this game round the table, making use of walnuts from the dessert course.

To begin, each player takes a walnut in his right hand. Everyone joins in the rhythmic incantation, "La-Di-Da."

FIRST PART: On the words "La" and "Di," the players merely thump the walnut on the table in front of them. On the word "Da," however, each player passes the nut to the person on his right and lets go of it.

SECOND PART: Each player takes the nut, which has been passed, in his right hand. He repeats the first part, passing the nut to the right and letting go of it on "Da."

THIRD PART: This gets more difficult now! The rhythmic incantation becomes "La-Di-Da-Di-Da-Di-Da." Each player takes the nut which has been passed to him in the right hand. The nut is thumped to the right on "La," then over to the left on "Di"; back to the right on "Da" (don't let go this time); to the left on "Di," to the right on "Da" (don't let go yet), to the left on "Di," to the right again on the final "Da" and *this* time the nut is passed to the right and let go of as before.

Repeat the whole thing from the beginning and go on through the sequence without stopping, making the tempo faster and faster.

If played properly, there should be a constant movement of nuts around the players in a counter-clockwise direction, with each strike of the table in absolute time, and a fluidity of movement which will be a joy to behold. (In reality, there will be nuts flying all over the place. One player will inevitably end up with a huge collection, and the game will end in chaos, which is much more fun, really!)

Yes and No

One player thinks of some person or thing, and the others ask questions about it. "Is it animal, vegetable, or mineral?" "Is it alive?" "Does it have two legs or four?" "Is it edible?" The only answer he can give is "Yes" or "No." The inquirers must guess what he is thinking from his answers. Shrewd questions will soon lead to discovery.

The player who guesses correctly must then think of some person or thing, and questioning starts again.

"It was a Game called Yes and No,
where Scrooge's nephew had to think of
something, and the rest must
find out what; he only answering to their
questions yes or no as the case was."

A Christmas Carol

"*Next morning he evinced an
unusual attachment
to silence and soda water.*"

— Charles Dickens

A Cure For Overeating and Overdrinking

tablespoon of Angostura bitters
1/2 pint of soda water

Mix.

Fresh Fruit Compote

pineapple, medium-size
4 pears
4 apples
4 plums
bunch of grapes
icing sugar, to taste
2 tablespoons of brandy
2 tablespoons of lemon juice
1/4 bottle of champagne, chilled

(Continued on following page)

1. Peel, core, and slice pineapple into
   rings, reserving the top.
2. Slice each pineapple ring in half.
3. Peel, core, and slice pears and apples.
4. Slice plums, and halve grapes.
5. Dust with icing sugar to taste.
6. Mix fruit together.
7. Moisten with brandy and lemon juice.
8. Toss well, and chill.

Just before serving, transfer to a serving
bowl. Pour over champagne. Decorate
with pineapple top.

This is a good start to breakfast.

Yield: 4 to 6 servings

Bubble and Squeak

onion, medium-size
a little bacon fat
4 rashers of streaky bacon
3/4 pound of cold mashed potatoes
ounce of butter
1/4 pound of chopped cooked cabbage
salt and black pepper
nutmeg, freshly ground

1. Finely chop the onion, and sauté it in bacon fat until transparent.
2. Push to one side of the skillet.
3. Remove rind of bacon, chop and fry until cooked, but not brown.
4. Push to one side with the onions.
5. Add mashed potatoes to the bacon fat, and warm through.
6. Put onion and bacon on top of potatoes, and push to one side.

(Continued on following page)

7. Add butter to pan, melt, and add cabbage, pepper, salt and nutmeg.
8. Stir well.
9. When thoroughly hot, pile on top of potatoes, bacon and onions.
10. Spread and flatten out the mixture over the entire pan, allowing the bottom to become brown and crisp.

When serving, turn out so that it is crispy side up.

This very old-fashioned dish gets its whimsical name from the potatoes that bubble and the cabbage that squeaks! It is delicious served with grilled bacon and eggs.

Yield: 4 servings

*"... announcement that the baby
had been taken in the act of putting a doll's
frying-pan into his mouth, and
was more suspected of having swallowed a
fictitious turkey, glued on a wooden
platter! The immense relief of finding this a
false alarm! The joy, and gratitude,
and ecstasy!"*

∾

*"Really, for a man who had been
out of practice for so many years, it was a
splendid laugh, a most illustrious
laugh. The father of a long, long line of
brilliant laughs!"*

A Christmas Carol

Glossary

<u>Terms</u>	<u>Word Meanings</u>
caster sugar	superfine sugar
egg, size 3	medium-size egg
jelly bag	bag for straining foods cooked with sugar
loaf sugar	hard sugar
rasher of bacon	several thin slices
sippets	small bit of toast
soured cream	sour cream
tot	a small allowance of liquor

Conversion Table

These conversions are approximate, but standard equivalents.

<u>British</u>   <u>American</u>

Oven Temperature

Cool	150 - 225° Fahrenheit
Slow	250 - 300°
Moderate	325 - 350°
Fairly hot	375 - 400°
Hot	425 - 450°
Very hot	475 - 550°

Measurements

pound of fat	2 cups
pound of flour	4 cups
pound of sugar	2 cups
pound of cheese, grated	4 cups
pound of fruit, dried	3 cups
8 ounces, liquid	cup (1/2 pint)
10 ounces (1/2 pint)	1 1/4 cups
20 ounces (1 pint)	2 1/2 cups
tablespoon	1 1/4 tablespoons
teaspoon	1 1/4 teaspoons

Bibliography

Dexter, Walter (ed.). *The Letters of Charles Dickens*. Nonesuch Press, 1938.

Forster, John. *The Life of Charles Dickens*, vol. 2. J.P. Lippincott & Co., 1874.

An Afternoon with Cedric Charles Dickens. Audio cassette. The Belvedere Press, 1992.

~

The abridged version of *A Christmas Carol* is available for purchase from The Dickens House Museum, 48 Doughty Street, London WC1N 2LF. Charles Dickens edited the text himself for his public readings. Designed for reading aloud, it takes approximately one hour.

A Note to the Programme Reader

The Reader should read Introduction to the Evening (page 28) and this note to follow in preparation for the evening's programme.

Charles Dickens is beloved as an author, and he was, also, a talented actor. In writing stories, he heard in his mind the sound of the words that he was putting down on paper. This is why Dickens' words lend themselves readily to being read aloud and why so many people enjoy hearing them.

What more can a Reader wish for than the clear description of the character of Ebenezer Scrooge: " . . . a squeezing, wrenching, grasping, scraping, clutching, covetous old sinner! Hard and sharp as flint, from which no steel had ever struck out generous fire; secret and self-contained, and solitary as an oyster . . . ."

With such exciting words at his disposal, the Reader can reach his audience's feelings much as a violinist reaches his listeners. A slight inflection of the voice, an appropriate expression of the face, and the Reader brings a character to life. The fortunate Reader will be credited by the audience with powers he hardly knew he possessed. When asked how he makes himself look like such and such a character, the Reader can honestly reply: "Dickens did it." The Reader has only to grasp the opportunity.

Any Reader worth his salt will recognize Scrooge as theatrical "jam", a ready-made character part, with comedy and melodrama mixed by the hand of an expert. One can hardly go wrong. Scrooge at the end, however, is a far more difficult proposition. The Reader must keep up the bubbling, hysterical, enthusiasm of the old man, quite childish but sincere, playing it all at a high level and on one level, as it were. Scrooge's transformation can only be convincing, however, if the proper degrees of gradual remorse have been maintained during the transitional period. Each encounter with the three Ghosts must make its mark and must be apparent. Furthermore, Scrooge must not go back one step once an effect is shown. He must go on until he is ready for the final climax of humility and contrition: "Spirit! . . . Hear me. I am not the man I was. I will not be the man I must have been . . ." The end will then be convincing. If he has presented the whole thing correctly, the Reader will feel both exhilarated and exhausted.

This then is the particular challenge of reading the *Carol*. Like reading any of Dickens aloud, the Reader must strive to recreate the original thoughts of the writer and to recapture the thrill he must have experienced as he watched characters and scenes unfold on the blank page before him. The Reader's particular reward is to know that *A Christmas Carol* was Dickens' favourite story. He included it in his first public reading and kept it in his repertoire until the very last.

The Reader must imagine reading it to family or friends around the fireside. He must see the shadowy light of candles and flickering firelight, feel the warmth and friendliness. In that imagined atmosphere, the Reader will reach the hearts of his listeners, and the real spirit of Christmas will abound.

Index
Recipes by Courses

Index

A Note about the Authors

Charles Dickens at 47

Cedric and Elizabeth Dickens

Cedric Charles Dickens, great-grandson of Charles Dickens, was educated at Eton and Cambridge. During World War II, he served in the Royal Navy, where he met Elizabeth, a Navy driver. They married in 1948.

A corporate executive most of his life, he retired as Director of Communications with International Computers.

His first book, *Drinking with Dickens*, appeared in 1980. Four years later, *Dining with Dickens*, was published.

He is a director of the Dickens Inn in Philadelphia.

The couple has two children and three granddaughters. They live in Somerset, England.

David and Betty Dickens

David Dickens, great-grandson of Charles Dickens, served in the Royal Navy during World War II.

He and his wife Betty met early in their book-publishing careers. He retired after 40 years. She retired recently, having returned to book publishing after the birth of their two daughters and two sons.

His first collaboration with Cedric Dickens, his cousin, was on an edited reading version of *A Christmas Carol* in 1965. Proceeds from that book benefited The Dickens House Museum in London.

The Dickens have eight grandchildren. They live in East Sussex, England.

Design by Viviane Silverman, *Quicksilver Design*

Printing by Quebecor Printing Fairfield, Inc.

Line engravings, courtesy of Rare Book Department,
The Free Library of Philadelphia

Photography by Studio Lux